MW01248787

NEVER JUDGE A BOOK BY ITS COLOR

[Clean Version]

By Unique Coles

Contact Information:
(Cell) 1-641-715-3900 ext. 91581
www.bloodypoetry4uni.com
www.bloodypoetry4uni@yahoo.com
Facebook: http://www.facebook.com/justuniek
Twitter: @justuniek

Creative Consultant/Marketing
Omar Wilkerson
oglorious@hotmail
Cover Designer/Editor
Tony LaSala
sobe2tone@yahoo.com
Publishing Consultant
Deborah Smart
dmsmart@gladstonepublishing.com

Printed in United States of America

ISBN-13: 978-1463557249
ISBN-10: 1-463557-24-8

Special Thanks to:

Omar Wilkerson
&
Sondra Pressley

DEDICATION

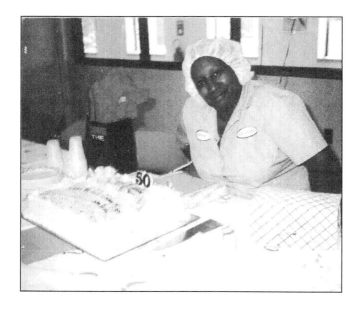

Delores Coles (8-29-1943 to 10-21-1999)

Mom's Special Occasion

The following letters were written from Mrs. Coles four sons; two at the time of her death in 1999, and two ten years later.

Dear Mom,

Life has Never been the same for me since that day- I try Not to recall that solemn day..... as i sat there with my father in a cold empty hospital waiting room as the doctor walked into the room, the nurse was tearing up, and the news was announced, ...aaaahhhhh, my breath escaped me, my eyes glazed with darkness, my soul felt empty and my heart paused, only for Me to gasp for a whisper of air, shhhhhh....what did you say i heard my father reply.....in like a film, my ears numbed by the repeated news; zoned in visible silence the ride away from the hospital was a moment that will live in my emptied soul forever; the street signs, the traffic lights, the ambience from the outside world seemed frozen in time,......some say that time heals all wounds...well like a opening in an unclosed hole (soul) mine hasn't healed, it's simply bandaged!

Love always,

Your oldest
10-21-2010

Hello Mom,

It's your next to the oldest. Can I talk with you for a minute? I know you're kind of busy right now with all of your friends and family; smiling and crying and talking about some of the good old times but I have a few things that I need to say to you. But before I get into it, guess who I saw today? I saw my father. It seems as if I was looking in the mirror because we look so much alike. You sure did pick a winner in him. Can't you see him smiling right now? He told me today that he just lost his best friend, and the pain in his voice and his eyes told me what I always needed to know. That is that he loved you more than life itself. Remember how I always called him Al Green? Truthfully speaking I got it from Keisha, but I can definitely see how he is so full of soul and I guess you are his Aretha Franklin, the queen of soul. Can you see all the people who came to see you tonight? You touched a lot of people lives with your beauty and grace. If your life can be

summed up in one word, I would have to say
"sincerity." You were sincere in your words, you
were sincere in your heart indeed, but most of all, you
were sincere in your belief in God. I know you would
like me to be a strong man, but you mean everything
to me and now it seems like I have nothing. People
tell me to just hold on and the wounds will heal on its
own. But I don't care if I have to cry for the rest of my
life because each tear will be a reminder of how much
I love you. I will never stop thinking about the
woman that gave me life, a father, 3 beautiful brothers
and unconditional love. Hold on Mom, I'm almost
finished. I don't want to take up everybody's time but
can I ask you a question? Why did you have to leave
us like this? I am in so much pain that I can do
nothing. I need you Mom. You were the picture of
how to love and of how to smile. You were my calm
after the storm. I'm not writing this letter to say
goodbye. I will never leave you and you will never
leave me. I'm writing to say hello. Hello Mom. How
are you doing today? Are you alright? That's good to
know. I'm sorry for any pain that I may have caused
you. I hope you will forgive me. So we are all here
today to pay our respect to who I believe is the most

appreciated and honest woman I ever met. Now, you
will shine like the sun forever. I love you Mom
yesterday, today and tomorrow

Love always,

Your next to the oldest
10-21-1999

"Talking to my mother"
I would like for this to be read during my mother's
eulogy.
I respectfully ask that my words be read
as they are written.

They say that children are suppose to bury their parents, but as far back as I can remember I always hoped that I would leave this world before my mother. My mother carried me close to her heart for nine months. I remember my mother telling me one day that when she was giving birth to me it was the hardest because I acted like I didn't want to come out. I guess that's because I knew that someday God would take her away from me. The lost of my mother is the hardest and most difficult thing that me and my family ever had to deal with, but I know that my mother did not suffer in death and I know that she is looking down from Heaven smiling on us. My mother's favorite word was to be strong, and I know that she is still saying that to all of us. My mother was a very religious, church going, God fearing woman all of her life. I know my mother's an angel now. God called her home to give her her wings. Now she is with her mother and her sisters.

My mother was such a loving woman. She loved us unconditionally. She was very understanding and sensitive. She was a giving person and always willing to help others. My mother loved to do things to bring a smile to someone's face. She got joy out of others happiness. She was respected by those who knew her. I never heard my mother utter a harsh word about anyone. I guess God saw that my mother was too good of a person to continue to live in this world, so he called her home to receive her wings. I know she's looking down at all the people who came out to pay their last respect. I know she's overwhelmed by all the love and wishes. I know she misses us, but I know she's telling us that she's okay. She's with her father now and for us to be strong and live a long and happy life.

I'm not a very religious person, but I believe in God and I accepted the Lord Jesus Christ as my savior. I know that today will be the last time that I would see my mother, so I got down on my knees for *the first time in so many years and prayed and cried and prayed and cried. I begged for God to give me the strength to be strong. When I got up from my knees, I knew my mother would*

always be with me. She will be in my heart forever. They say time heals all wounds and mends a broken heart. I was as close to my mother as a son could be and I will mourn the lost of my mother until I join her. This is whether my tears are of joy or sadness. To my father, brothers, nieces, nephews and the three grandchildren: Rahjohn, Hasmeek and Byseem; know that your wife, mother and grandmother loved us and will continue to love us very much. And I know that she wants our family to stay close and love one another and help one another the same as we did when she was with us. I love you Mommy. Please watch over us and keep us strong. I'll miss you so much.

Love always,

Your next to the youngest
10-21-1999

Dear Mom,

    I never was able to build up enough of nerve to write you this letter, but now I think it's time. Because I feel like this is the only way I can put the past behind. 1999 is a year that will always stick out in my head. Because that was the year I heard the worse words in my life, "She's dead." My worst nightmare has finally come true. I have faced my biggest fear in this world. Nothing has ever been more frightening to me than to losing my # 1 girl. I always imagined how it'll feel if we ever departed. But now I don't have to imagine no more, I never been so broken hearted. It's hard to explain that kind of pain, words just cannot describe it. It's the kind of pain that shows in your eyes, no matter how much you try to hide it. It's the kind of pain that doesn't go away, it's with you every night and day. Nothing or no one can make you feel better no matter what they do or say. But I have to move on I have to be strong at least for the sake of my kids. You have lived your life to the fullest so now it's my time to live. Although you may be gone physically, spiritually you're still alive. Your name lives on, you'll never be gone. I'll see you on the other side.

Love always,

Your youngest
10-21-2010

Never Judge A Book By Its Color

Cast of Characters

Main character

Unique – Poet/Rapper
Delores Coles- Unique's deceased Mother

Supportive Characters

LC-Unique's oldest brother/video director
Complete- Unique's next to the oldest/ "BIG BRO"/ex con
Hasheem- Unique's next to the youngest brother/ex con
Kevin- Unique's white brother from another mother
Family- Unique's nieces and nephews
Buke- Unique's nephew
Baby- Buke's baby
Janine- Unique's cousin
Mooky- Janine's daughter
Wanda- Unique's cousin
Uncle Robert- Unique's uncle
Ken Dawg- Unique's cousin
Shawn- Unique's cousin
Bridgette- friend of family/Re-al and Just's sister
Cousin Man- Unique's cousin
Re-al- family friend/Bridgette and Just's brother

Just- friend of family/Re-al and Bridgette's brother's

Assata- Complete's daughter

Regina- the mother of Hasheem's kids

Debo- shoplifter (booster) Unique's cousin

Mona- Unique's niece

Lina- Unique's niece

Baby Moms- The mother of Complete's kids

Ty-Ron- Complete's son

Shavonna- Unique's daughter

Unika- Unique's daughter

Daddy- Unique's father

New wife- Unique's step moms

Poetry Cast

What's Love- played by Omar's daughter *Monet and* and nephew *R'leymont*

Your Secret Admirer played by *Aja*- Unique's girlfriend

Why Does A Woman Cheat? Played by *Aja and Shaheem*

Your Are Not Alone played by *Heather* ex addict

Who Can I Turn To (Lost and Found) played by *Unique and Omar*

Table of Contents

WHO'S MY BROTHER?

When I speak of my **brother,**
I'm not speaking of my biological **brother.**
He's my brother by nature;
we both have the same mother.
The **brother** that I'm speaking of
is in the heart
and in the soul
Also is in the mind
which is self controlled
Just because of our same color
that doesn't makes you my **brother**
It's more to it than that
it's more than just being black
Brother hood it comes from within
not just judged by your skin
so if you think your my brother
because of your color
it's time you think again

WHO'S MY BROTHER?

BIG BRO

Dear Big Bro,

     A lot of the things has changed since...

well you know when.

Family gatherings,

they no longer be happening. We only see each other every now and then.

Hasheem?

Still living out in Paterson, you know, living the street life.

Maaan, things dun got crazy,

Buke

dun had a

baby,

and oh

Daddy,

he's got a

new wife.

I was the best man at his wedding,

and my blessings,
goes out to them both.
Although we're not close
like we use to be,
it's cool with me;
life goes on......

Remember cousin

Janine

that use to live around the way?
I just recently found out through
the grapevine
that her daughter

Mooky

was gay.
That's crazy!

Haven't heard from

Wanda

in a while,
probably somewhere knocked up.

Uncle Robert

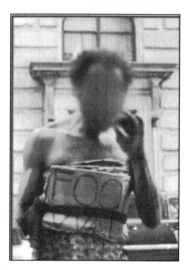

still smoking crack,

Ken-Dawg and Shawn

both locked

up.

Teresa sister

Bridget

was missingand it took a whole week just to find her.

Cousin Man

dun robbed this dude for 8 G's
and moved down to North Carolina,
but I think he's back though.
Oh,

Re-al

got locked up again,
more time wasted.
Up in the county but now he's back out.
Feds got 'em on an ankle bracelet.

Don't know what's up with his brother

Just,

but I do have to admit I kind of miss'em.
Last that I did hear, he was somewhere,
up in there lost up in the system.
This world is crazy!
Winters are getting colder,
summers are getting hotter.
It's been about two years since I have last
seen your daughter,

Assata.

I really do miss all of my

nieces and nephews--.

God knows how much I love'em.

Hass and Regina

dun lost the kids now, her moms got custody of
'em.
What a shame.
I'm really feeling his pain,
I know that's gotta be hard.

Debo

just got out, got
locked back up again.
Dun caught another boosting charge.
That's that city for you.
I gotta admit though,
I kind of missed that city flow.
Since

LC

been living down here,
he hadn't shot too many videos.
Business is slow.

But see, that's how it go,
when you're in the entertainment biz.
But other than that, his family's alright,
and

the kids

dun got maaad big.

Mona and Lina

are now at that age where they're really starting
to shine.

I don't remember the last time
I seen your

baby moms

or either your son

Ty-Ron

but I hope they're good.

The hood...

has changed. Now, everybody is into gangs.
"No love if you're not Blood"
and "Stay with a click when you're Crip".
God help us.

Back to family,

last time I seen my daughters

I was still living in New York.
Can you believe after all of that money
I dun sent down there
that year
I'm still paying for child support?
My youngest daughter Unika is 8
and my oldest daughter Shavonna is now 10.
This is just a brief summary
on how family and friends has been.
I hope you liked that,
and I hope you write back.

Peace!
11-28-2002

BIG BRO

BIG BRO

Dear Big Bro,

A lot of the things has changed since... well you know when. Family gatherings, they no longer be happening. We only see each other every now and then. Hasheem? Still living out in Paterson, you know, living the street life. Maaan, things dun got crazy, Buke dun had a baby, and oh Daddy, he's got a new wife. I was the best man at his wedding, my blessings, goes out to them both. Although we're not close like we use to be, it's cool with me; life goes on......Remember cousin Janine that use to live around the way? I just recently found out through the grapevine that her daughter Mooky was gay.

That's crazy! Haven't heard from Wanda in a while, probably somewhere knocked up. Uncle Robert still smoking crack, Ken-Dawg and Shawn both locked up. Teresa sister Bridget was missing and it took a whole week just to find her. Cousin Man dun robbed this dude for 8 G's and moved down to North Carolina, but I think he's back though. Oh, Re-al got locked up again, more time wasted. Up in the county but now he's back out. Feds got 'em on an ankle bracelet. Don't know what's up with his brother Just, but I do have to admit I kind of miss 'em. Last that I did hear, he was somewhere, up in there lost up in the system.

This world is crazy! Winters are getting colder, summers are getting hotter. It's been about two years since I have last seen your daughter, Assata. I really do miss all of my nieces and nephews-God knows how much I love'em. Hass and Regina dun lost the kids now, her moms got custody of 'em. What a shame. I'm really feeling his pain, I know that's gotta be hard.

Debo just got out, got locked back up again. Dun caught another boosting charge. That's that city for you. I gotta admit though, I kind of missed that city flow. Since LC been living down here, he hadn't shot too many videos. Business is slow. But see, that's how it go, when you're in the entertainment biz. But other than that, his family's alright, and the kids dun got maaad big. Mona and Lina are now at that age where they're really starting to shine. I don't remember the last time I seen your baby moms or either your son Ty-Ron, but I hope they're good.

The hood... has changed. Now, everybody is into gangs. "No love if you're not Blood" and "Stay with a click when you're Crip". God help us.

Back to family, last time I seen my daughters I was still living in New York. Can you believe after all of that money I dun sent down there that year I'm still paying for child support?

My youngest daughter Unika is 8 and my oldest daughter Shavonna is now 10. This is just a brief summary on how family and friends has been. I hope you liked that, and I hope you write back.

Peace!
11-28-2002

I'M CHANGING MY LAST NAME

A letter to my father
On October 21,1999 I lost my best friend in this
world, my mother;
And not too long after losing my mother
I have soon discovered
That the last person who I had in this world
who I thought that I can depend on
Has done me wrong
and treated me as if I was never born
Just be strong you say,
hey;
easier said than done
When your moms passed on
and now your father
treats you like you're not
his son,
What did I do to deserve
this ?
I showed this man nothing
but love,
Is he now repaying me back
from all of the things that I did
when I was out there
dealing with them drugs?
Or could it be
that he never did like me
and it was all just a big
front?

Doing all of these fatherly things
only cause he knows that,
that's what mom dukes would want.
But now she's *she's* no longer here
and he
he no longer cares
and we
we no longer share
nothing together,
now it's whatever.
I'll hear from you whenever I hear from you
and I'll see you when I see you;
but your a grown man now
so I will no longer
house you, cloth you or feed you;
You're right pops
I am a grown man
and
I can provide for myself but
I still like to know
that I have a father that cares
now is that asking for too much?
Well, obviously it is
I hope I'm not the way you are with my kids
when they start to get older
and the world gets harder
and seems to get
just a bit
colder,
They will always no

that no matter what,
I will always be there
To wipe away all of their
tears
and help them face their
biggest fears;
Show them unconditional
love
cause
blood
is all we have
Don't you know that when
you hurt I hurt
and when you're mad I'm mad?
We eat together
we sleep together
we're family
we're peeps forever,
Now, that's the true definition of family,
although you may not understand me,
Understand this;
This poem will be the last time
you ever hear from me
And rather you would want it this way or not,
now this is how it has to be,
so
so long
have a happy life
and I'll try to do the same
And to show you how serious I am about this

I'M CHANGING MY LAST NAME!

This poem was written when I was going

through some troubling times in my life.

It was the way I felt at that time.

There are no hard feelings

between me and my dad.

We have a great relationship

and just for the record,
I do love him dearly.

I Watched You Grow

A letter from my father

I watched you grow, *I knew you before you even knew yourself*

W*hy when you hurt instead of coming to me*
  you go to everyone else?
A*ll of your life, I've always been there*
  don't you know I'll never leave you?
T*rust me, I'm on your side*
  and I'll never mislead you
C*ome to me when you're having problems*
  and you'll see how quick I can solve them
H*ave a little more trust in me*
  and your troubles would no longer be
E*very day I watch you grow*
  and I watch what you do
D*o you know how wrong it is*
  for you to be so untrue?

Y*ou surprises me at times*
  because I know what is in your heart
O*thers may think that you're dumb*
  but I know you and I know that you're smart
U*nfortunately, you don't use what you have to your advantage*

God gave you a brain to use
  why you don't use it, I don't understand it
Remember what I'm telling you
  because I'll never tell you a lie
Open up your eyes
  because too much is passing you by
W hen you need someone to talk to
  and you don't know where else to go
  Come and talk to me, I'm your father **I WATCHED YOU GROW**

"HEAVENLY FATHER THAT IS..."

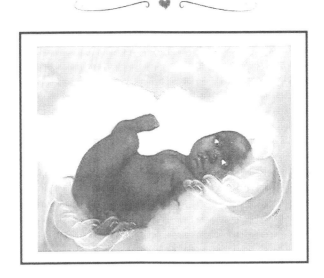

Thank You

Thank you so very much
   for being there when I need you
How can I ever repay you back
   and what can I do to please you?
And make you see how much I appreciate
   all that you've done
Never will I forget the one
   who treated me like a son
Knowing you're there for me takes a lot of stress off my chest

You're the reason I'm at peace
   when I lay my head to rest
Out of all the other people I know
   and who I thought really cared
Unfortunately, they forgot all about me but I **THANK YOU** God for
   being there

WHAT DO YOU BELIEVE IN?
WHAT DO YOU BELIEVE IN?

What do you believe in?
     Do you believe in God?
He who do more power to you
     but now lets take a ride
And find out if there's really a God
     or is it just a myth
The way things are looking now a day if there is a God
     he must be pissed

Do you believe in Satan
     and the powers he's known to have?
Or do you believe we're here by mistake and just
     waiting for time to pass?

You should believe in something
     other than what the physical eyes can see
Other than yourself tell me who else
     do you believe can set you free?
Up in Heavens there's Angels and in Hell there's
     demons; that's what they say

But what in heaven the hell is this
        on earth that's here everyday?
Erase away all of the bad things
        and how would this world be?
Like Heaven I assume but not no room
        for people like you and me
If you don't believe in Heaven or Hell
        than what is your belief?
Eternity on earth, coming back to birth,
        living in this world in peace?
Very few people live their lives
        not believing in something
Even if they just believe in a rock it's better than
        believing in nothing

It's up to you to believe in what's true
        but believe in it for the right reasons
Now, let me ask you again, **WHAT DO YOU
        BELIEVE IN?**

WHAT IF?

What if there wasn't any drugs in the world
whAt would this world be like?
It'll probably be like Heaven no crimes,
no killings or no fights
What if there wasn't any racism
how would people in the world act?
They'll probably would show more love for one
another rather they we're white or black
What if there was a cure for aids and
it wasn't such a threat?
There probably wouldn't be so many people dying
or practicing having safe sex
What if there wasn't any money in the world
and we all can live for free?
What if we all can live together forever in
perfect harmony?
What if everyone spoke the truth and
no one told a lie?
What if time just stood still and
never passed us by?

What if there wasn't any religions and
we all had the same belief?
What if we all just got along and
lived in this world in peace?
What if the world was here alone and
people didn't exist?

And **what if** we decide when we
died?

Now that's a **BIG WHAT IF!**

MY NIKES

I hear ambulance sirens, I see cops flying,
like someone's dying
I walk down the street and I notice
a whole crowd of people crying
So I make my way through the crowd
you know,
just to see what could it be
That was making these people cry like this
and it was such a tragedy
Right in front of my eyes lies
a young black man on the streets
In a puddle of blood,
with nothing on his feet
At 1st I thought, that it must have been
a hit and run
But than I noticed the bullet holes
in his clothes
so he had to be shot with a gun;
But that still doesn't explain
whatever happened to my man sneakers;
So just out of curiosity
I started to dig a little deeper;
I asked around,
and than I found
out what really went down;

This young black man was gunned down
over a pair of kicks,
now ain't that a big trip !

BLOODY POETRY

Roses are red and violets are blue

that poem is old so here's something new;

Roses don't grow where I come from

the clouds are black and it covers the sun

Which darkens the city, make life look so gritty

Where everything's ugly that use to look pretty

I never seen violets, but I've seen violence

I'm drowned by the sound there's never no silence

I know this sounds harsh, but it is true

Roses are dead and violets are too.

REST IN PEACE

Rest in peace my friend
God bless your soul
Even though you're gone
the life you lived will still be told
Sorry you had to leave us
oh how I wish that you were still here
The day that I heard you passed away still fills my eyes with tears

I couldn't believe this happened
this could not be true
No way can my friend leave me like this with all we had left to do

Please tell me that I'm dreaming
and soon I'll awake
Even though I know we all have to go
this I just couldn't take
After all we've been through
I just couldn't accept your death

Cause of you, I've always been true
now my best friend has left
Every day to God I pray please take good care of my friend

REST IN PEACE
One love mom dukes
until we meet again

WHAT'S LOVE?

What: What is this thing called Love?
And where does it come from;
Does it come from the Heavens above?
Is Love something that you see,
Or is it something that you feel?
And if you are in Love
How do you know that it is for real?
I think that I am in Love but I don't know for sure

> **Love:** Love is not something that comes knocking at
> your door
> Love is in the heart; it's something you feel inside
> And once you are in Love it's a feeling you cannot
> hide

What: Well if I'm in love than tell me Love how would
I know it?

> **Love:** Like I said, you can't hide the feeling
> If you're in Love than you would show it

What: What should I do when Love finally comes my
way?
Should I reject it and run away,
Or should I accept it and stay?

Love: True Love only comes around once in a life time;
So just thank God that someone loves you,
And is always thinking of you

What: If Love doesn't love me back than what should I do?

Love: Then it must be lust because real Love would always be true

What: So I guess I do love you

Love: And Love loves you too.

10 Different Reasons Why I Love You

There's a million and one reasons why I love you but for now here's just 10

1. I love you for being my partner, for being my lover
and for being my girlfriend
2. I love you for you being you
and being true to thy self
3. I love you for hanging in there with me
and not leaving me all by myself
4. I love you for the inspiring things you say
and the encouraging things that you do
5. Hold on boo, I'm half way through,
with telling you 10 DIFFERENT
REASONS WHY I LOVE YOU
6. I love the way you walk, the way you talk,
your smile and your style
7. I love you for not running out on me
when I was out there running wild
8. I love you for you loving me
when I couldn't even love myself
9. I love you through good times, through bad times,
through sickness and through health
10. I love you to death do us part;
you'll always be in my heart forever
There's a million and one reasons why I love you
but this is just 10 that I just put together

P.S. Next year I'll give you 10 more reasons now, that's just 1 more reason for you
to stick around

YOUR SECRET ADMIRER

Girls as pretty as you
only comes around like every hundred years.
The day you were brought into this world
I still can hear the angels cheer
Hip hip hurray!
It's a baby girl!
The most beautiful thing in this world.
You know,
you're really something special,
God has truly blessed you.
I'm not psychic
but I predict
you have a man because only
A girl as pretty as yourself
never have to worry about being lonely.
Who ever the man maybe,
I wonder if he knows how lucky he is.
To have a girl as pretty as you,
is just more of a reason to live.
If I had 3 wishes in this world
this is what it'll be
1 to know you,
2 to love you
and you can imagine # 3

Who knows,
maybe in another world
or in another life.
I'll come back as a preacher
and you'll come back as my wife

Signed,

Yours if you want me to be
Your Secret Admirer

IF I COULD I WOULD

If I could I would
give you the world, cause girl
Lord knows you deserve it.
I don't mean to come off like every other guy
because I know that you already heard this,
If I could I would
wash away all of your troubles
with one snap of my finger;
I'm not a singer
But If I could I would
sing you a song
that'll last the whole night long;
There's nothing in this world
that I wouldn't do for you;
for you I would even die for;
If I could I would
take on all of your pain
so you won't have to cry no more
I'll wipe away all of your tears,
won't go nowhere,

I'll be right there to the bitter end
If I could I would
die in your arms,
come back just to die all over again
Because in your arms forever is where I wanna be
baby I'm gonna be
straight up with you
You're the best thing that ever happened to me so,
even if I could I would...
never let you go

MY HEART IS IN
THE PALM OF YOUR HANDS

♫ *You love me, you complete me*
♫ *You hold my heart in your hand*

Every time I hear that song by Keisha Cole,
I think about where we stand,
My heart has been broken before
and it's just beginning to heal;
I don't ever wanna feel
that kind of pain again,
so now that I've let you in,
Please be careful with what you do to my heart
while it's in the palm of your hands;
I'm a strong man
but another heart break
Is something I don't think I can take
Although I know
that you're not out to hurt me
I just want you to understand
That I've let my guards down
and now…

My Heart Is In The Palm Of Your Hands

GOOD KNOWING YOU

Dear girlfriend.

The time has come for me to say that I must be on my way. Although, what we had was good in this relationship.. I no longer can stay. Since I've been away from what they so call the real world. I've been all alone I've been on my own; whatever happened to my so-called girl? No need to explain because the games you played will no longer be played with me, cause see, enough is enough, and now my mind has been made. No more will I worry about if you're out there having sex; Cause now you're just an ex, and like you, there will be a next. No need to feel sorry for me, cause see, I'll be just fine. By the time I finish this letter, your name will be erased from my mind. Everything that's in my past, I'm leaving it there and I'm starting fresh. I schooled you when I was home; when I went to jail you failed the test. You must've forgotten about all of the things that I've been showing you. So now I must say good bye what - cha - ma - call - it, it's been GOOD KNOWING YOU

GOOD KNOWING YOU

WHY DOES A WOMAN CHEAT?

From a man's prospective

For every man there's a woman; for every woman there's a man (**N Y C**)

Most women are loyal; most men will cheat every chance they can (**N Y C**)

It's a man's ego that makes him behave the way that he do (**N Y C**)

Most men are greedy; they like to have their cake and eat it too (**N Y C**)

When a man cheats on a woman, he makes it seems like it's all right (**N Y C**)

But when a woman cheats on a man, he wants to argue, fuss and fight (**N Y C**)
If a woman isn't satisfied, that's a reason for her to cheat (**N Y C**)
If she's not getting what she wants at home, she'll get it out on the streets (**N Y C**)
Because a woman has needs and they need to be fulfilled (**N Y C**)
If you're not fulfilling her needs, than somebody else will (**N Y C**)
She'll find another who can satisfy her emotional and physical needs (**N Y C**)
If she loves you she'll just cheat on you, rather than up and leave (**N Y C**)
Because like a man, a woman like to have their cake and eat it too (**N Y C**)
But they don't cheat because of their ego, they cheat because they don't know what else to do (**N Y C**)
As a man do what you suppose to do and you won't have to be over protective
These are a few reasons why a woman cheats from a man's prospective

*If you answered **N** to 3 or more of these questions than you're probably a female*

*If you answered **Y** to most of these questions than you're probably a male*

*If you answered **C** to any of these questions than you're probably confused and you're probably from*

N
Y
C
(GET IT?) LOL

NEVER TRUST A BIG BUTT
AND A SMILE

Every girl with a big butt and a smile
believe me you can't trust
Just because she might look good
that doesn't means she's got good stuff,
She's probably been had,
by every son and dad,
that lives around the block;
And what she's got
she's gladly giving it away,
and you don't have to pay
Because the price
is your life
which is worth more than money;
It's funny,
how a big butt and a smile
can attract you like bees to honey.
This girl that I knew who looked very pretty
and had a big butt and a smile
Was HIV
and having sex

like it was going out of style;
She once met this guy
as she was walking by
whom she never seen before
And that same day
not a day later
she was at his front door,
And instead of him finding out
if this girl was straight
he just couldn't wait
So he sexed her
without even using a rubber,
I really feel for this brother
Because of him putting all of this trust
in this big butt filled with lust,
Now it's ashes to ashes
and dust to dust
a BIG BUTT and a smile you can't trust

WHY A MAN CRY?

Why a man cry,
　　　　is this a normal thing to do?
He cries because he's tired
　　　　of all the madness that he goes through
You go through so much in life
　　　　you have no other choice but to cry

After suffering all of your life
　　　　then you have to turn around and die

My mother brought me into this world
　　　　I didn't ask to be here
And if it was up to me
　　　　I'll turn back the time and disappear
Never say a man isn't suppose to cry
　　　　because he has every right

Crying is good for the soul,
　　　　so my pain I no longer fight
Remember when you're hurting so much inside
　　　　and you feel like you can just die
You're a man but you're still only human
　　　　so you have the right to cry

LIVING IN THE DRUG WORLD

Living in the drug world it's a world filled with
loneliness and sorrow.
Today if you think that you had it bad, it only
gets worse tomorrow.
Over and over you keep asking yourself how did
I ever end up here?
You try to escape from it but no matter how fast
you run you're going nowhere.
Around and around in circles you go keep ending
up in the same spot;
Doing things you never imagined of doing,
running and hiding from cops.
The kids that you once knew and went to school
with over the years,
have all moved on; are all long gone, are working
and have careers.
The friends that you use to have, now look at
you
and laugh;

consider you nothing but trash, talk bad about you
every time you walk pass.
Your own family disowns you; wish they never
known you,
when over the years nothing but love was all that
they've ever shown you.
But because of the drugs, you lost their love, now out
of the house they've thrown you.
Now all night you wander the streets,
with nowhere to sleep
and nothing to eat.
And the socks you have on your feet,
you had on for the last past week.
No one no longer respects you.
Your baby moms wish she never met you.
You want to give your baby a hug but because of
how you look, the mother won't let you.

You been in and out of rehabs
for about the last past 10 years.
And keep going back to dope and crack
because you feel like no one cares.
And after every high you start telling yourself,
this is it!
This time, I'm serious, I swear to God,
I'm going to quit!
And the very next chance you get
you're right back at it.
You refuse to admit that you have a problem
or that you are an addict.
Addicted to drugs and madly in love with just
the thought of getting high;
If you were giving the choice to live sober or die
getting high, you'll rather die.
So if you want to die from getting high, just
make sure you are prepared.

Because death is right around the corner
and you're almost there.
But if for any reason you decide you want to live
long and strong;
Then leave that life you're living behind
and start singing a brand-new song.

FREE AT LAST, FREE AT LAST, THANK GOD ALMIGHTY I AM FREE AT LAST!!!

The Difference Between You and Me

We all are created equal
but we all are not the
same;
The difference between
you and me
just isn't in our names;
You react before you think,
other than you, I think before I react
I use my head instead,
instead you choose to use a gun or a bat
You'd rather sell drugs for a living
I'd rather work and get mines the honest
way
I come in peace.
you carry a piece.
I'm serious while you play;
The difference between you and me
is that you try to be like everyone else
But other than you
I stay true
and I always be myself;
You only can see what's in front of you;
I use my 3rd eye to see.
You over react:
I humble myself:
now that's THE DIFFERENCE BETWEEN
YOU AND ME

THE DIFFERENCE BETWEEN YOU AND ME

YOU ARE NOT ALONE

Y ou are not alone in this world there's people out
there just like you

O thers who suffer, and who goes through the
same pain as you do

U nderstand, you're not the only one in this world
who go through bad times

A lot of people go through their who life dumb,
deaf and blind

R emember when you think that you have it bad,
there's people worst off than you

E ating out of garbage cans, begging for money, not
even a home to go to

N o one like to go through bad time; that's just a
part of living

O ld and young, we all go through it; just give
thanks to God for giving

T he strength to you; for you to move on and put
the past behind

A nd later in life when things are looking up, you
can look back at these times

L ook at it like this, bad times doesn't last forever

O ver and over just keep telling yourself that soon
I'll get it together

N o one goes through life with ease; this is a fact
that is known

E ven when you're having bad times just remember
YOU ARE NOT ALONE

YOU ARE NOT ALONE

WHO CAN I TURN TO?

Lost and found

LOST: Who can I turn to when times are hard?
Should I turn to my mother, my father, or
should I turn to God?
It's kind of hard for me to turn to
someone who I can't physically see
How can someone who I can't see do
anything for me?
Just have faith you say but how much
faith must one have?

FOUND: Do you believe in God?

LOST: Maybe I do and why you ask?

        FOUND: Because if you do than you
                    should know that he is the one
                    to turn to
                    When times are hard, all you
                    need to do is talk to God

LOST: But how do I know if he's listening or
      not?

        FOUND: Believe me, he knows about the
                    problems that you got

LOST: Who can I turn to when my rights are
      being violated?
      Who can I turn to when my house is
      illegally raided?

        FOUND: No matter what happens in
                    life, or whatever you go
                    through, bottom line, God is
                    the only one who you could
                    turn to

WATCH'EM, HE'S TRICKY

I know this person who loves cursing
and who loves to rob and steal
And to kill another means nothing to him
so he'll gladly do it again,
At times he appears to be friendly
and approaches you with a greeting and smile
But don't be fooled by this person,
he'll get you the best way he knows how;
He talks to you like he's your best friend
even show you how to make fast money,
I use to give him whatever he wanted
but now he gets nothing from me
I'm on to his game, I see how he roll,
I see the things that he stole,
So he's not to be trusted no matter what
he's nothing but bad luck,
Just when things are looking up
and you're getting your foot off the ground,
Here he comes again doing all he can
in his powers to bring you back down;
Misery loves company, believe that this is true,

So Whenever you feel like you're being brought
down by this person here's what
you do...

Let us bow our heads

*"In Jesus name oh Heavenly Father I come to you
for strength and power to keep this person away
today I pray
Asking for you to come into my heart
and forgive me for my sins
I rebuke you Satan; in the name of Jesus, Amen"*

WHO ARE YOU WORKING FOR?

I once knew this kid who sold drugs for a living
and never had a job;
Was quick to rob,
grew up on the wild side,
and never believed in God;
Dropped out of school at the age of 12
and went to jail at the age of 13
Was out of control,
at 14 years old,
wearing a hand full of gold rings
Material things ruled his world
and girls
fail down at his feet
And you can tell by the way that he speak
that he was real smooth on the streets;
Didn't have much school knowledge
but was street smart,
he knew enough
To make it out on the streets alone
if things ever got too tough;
Had little respect for his parents

not to mention everyone else around him
And to those who downed him
in the past,
he now looks at them and laugh
And think because of his money
he's better than everyone else in the world
And his girl
was just a gold digger,
anyone with money she'll consider;
Living the street life 7 years
without taking a fall,
all looked lovely in his eyes;
by the age of 21 he had it all
Everything, accept the most important thing,
besides his money and rings,
there was something that was missing from his
life,
other than material things;
Which will soon be gone,
because to him it doesn't belong,
you see,

the devil, just let him hold it for a while
and than he take it and smile
Than after the devil done robbed what you robbed,
then you decide to go to God
Asking for all of these worldly things back,
spiritually still being attacked
By Satan, who's making you think
that your world is only based on money;
He let you do good for a while,
than he brings you back down,
because he think that it's funny
Your working for Satan;
the money you're making
on the corner every day
It all belongs to the evil one,
so he comes and he takes it away,
Now aren't you tired of starting all over
because you keep getting robbed?
You wanna make money
and keep making money?
Than come and work for God,

than come and work for God,

With that money your making,

you're working for Satan,

you need to come and work for God!

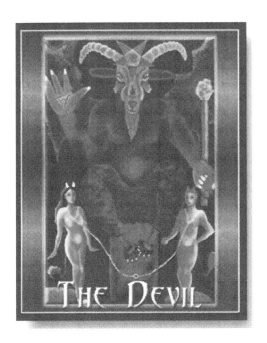

WHO AM I ?

W ho am I, I ask myself this question
  every day?
H ow can I find myself? Can I find me
  if I pray?
O h my precious Lord, I'm lost and I
  need some help

A t times I don't know who I am,
  please help me find myself
M any days I wonder would it matter
  to any one if I die

I can't go on like this Lord please tell
  me WHO AM I?

NY?

WHO AM I?

THE STORY OF THE PEOPLE
(essay)

Once upon a time some important people were fighting with one another. Each saying they were better than the other. The most powerful, the most useful, and the most *important:*

Doctor said:

I'm definitely the most important. I am the sign of life and hope. I was chosen to save all people. Without me all of the sick would die. Look all around the world and you will see all of the lives I've saved.

Fireman stepped in:

Pardon me; but why is it that you only think of the sick people? Think about the houses and the buildings they're living in. Fires are going on all over the world. So without me you'll have more than you can handle.

Comedian started laughing:

Ha ha ha. You both are buggin'! I bring laughter into the world. I bring tears of joy into all of the people's eyes. Every time you see me you are filled with joy and laughter. So without me there will be no more fun.

Teacher waved her hand and interrupted:

I'm filled with the most important thing in this world, 'knowledge.' Without me you all would be wasted. "And a mind is a terrible thing to waste." I don't socialize often; but when I enter a classroom my knowledge is so striking that no one gives any of you a second thought.

Policeman couldn't stand it any more- he shouted out:
Freeze! I have power over you all. I am here to protect and serve the people. Without me you'll all be killing yourselves. I am the law, and whenever one of you wishes to break the law I'll deal with you personally.

Judge finally took the stand:
My powers are even greater than those of a policeman. Doctors, firemen, comedians, teachers and even Mr. Policeman have to answer to me. I am the one who keeps them all out of jail. People do not question me, they listen and obey.

Mother spoke more quietly than all the others:

Think of me. I am the one who carried you for nine months. You hardly pay me any attention but without me none of you would be here. You need me for encouragement, love and support.

They all went on bragging. Each of them convinced they were the better one. Their yelling between each other became louder and louder.

Suddenly, there was a bright flash of lightening and a loud sound of thunder came about. A hurricane was approaching very heavily and strongly. The people all fell down in fear for their lives. This drew them all closer to one another for comfort. Then hurricane spoke…

Hurricane:

You foolish people. Fighting with one another. Each trying to overpower the other. Do you not know that God made all of you, each for a special reason? God loves all of you. So now join hands and come together as one. Because you are all loved, and you can all live together in peace.

So when God sends us a hurricane to bring us closer together we should remember that this is how he wants us to be.

Dedicated to all who were affected by Hurricane Katrina

WHAT IF? (LYRICS)
(Extended version)
The song

Verse 1

Sometimes I go into deep thoughts I mentally take trips
I start thinking and wondering about the what-ifs
like uhmmmm......
What if there wasn't no more drugs being made,
I wonder now how would drug dealers get paid?
Or if everyone said no to drugs and yes to God
now would they find another hustle, or try to find a job?
And to my sisters on the corners that selling that a..
I wonder what she would've been if she never took that blast
And got all strong out from the drugs that dealers been
selling her
Who knows she'll probably be the next Mrs. America
Doing her thing on stage getting paid
yo think about this
what if
there was a cure for Aids?
And it wasn't such a threat
it wouldn't be so many people practicing having safe sex
No more condoms, raw dogging, nothing but skin
The way we use to do, you know, way back when
When Aids wasn't around and the sex was great!
Before I run up in you raw now I'd rather master...wait!
(**hook**)
Think about this
what if
the world was here alone and people didn't exist
or if time stood still and never passed us by
or if we had a say so on our time to die
think about this
what if
the world was here alone
and people didn't exist......
and people didn't exist
yeah, now think about this

Verse 2

What if there wasn't any racism?
And the race we hate we lived under the same roof with
them
And the color of our skin was irrelevant
And every man was being judged by their intelligence
That's a day I'm hoping that I will soon see
when every one is giving the same opportunity
All people treated equal and under one race
And not judged because of the color of their face
What if
there wasn't any money and we all could live for free?
And working was an option than how would this world
be?
It'll be more chilling, less killing I would imagine
And we all got the same much so no need for bragging
What for, when we all go to the same store
And
nobody's rich
and
nobody's poor
On the same path and in the same class
and nobody is better,
yo dig we all in it together
forever one love no doubt
this is something at times that I think about
now
(hook)
Verse 3
What if everyone spoke the truth and no one told a lie?
And even if they tried they died
And got sent straight to hell I wonder if Heavens like that
Or if I was in Heaven can I still write raps?
And be a ghost writer and still making hits
doing songs with Tupac and Biggie
What if
everyone lived in peace,
under one religion and all had the same belief?
Together as one and one family under the sun

yo picture this son
What if
nobody had a gun?
Than the world a be over crowded evidently
No more parole and all the jail houses would be empty
Now all a cop got is a badge and flash light
No more pulling out now you have to fight
With your hands like a real man don't care if you big
dig
you lose some you win some but at least you get to live
another day to come back and fight again
So when you think about it you really did win
now
(hook)

Never Judge A Book By Its Color

Just the other day
this other man walked up to me and asked me
Why do you wear your hair like that
and why do you dress so tacky?
So I said
1st of all
what is it your concern
Is there something about my race my man
you're trying to learn?
Because if so,
that's not the way to go,
that's more of an invitation
for a brother like me to send you away
on an everlasting vacation.
And 2nd of all
I see nothing wrong with the way I'm dressed.
What I gotta wear a suit and tie or something
for me to be a success?
Pull out your pen and pad my man
this information I want you to gather
It's all about what's on the inside,
what's on the outside really doesn't matter.
You can have on a suit and tie
and I can have on boots untied
But does that make you a better man,
or means that you have better plans?
I think not!
And furthermore
how dare you talk about my hair,
Tell me something my man,
Is it what's on my head that you fear?
Because if so,
It's not what's on my head that you need to be so worried
about
You need to worry about what's inside of my head;
because that's what'll take you out.
Now,
write this down
for what I believe in
I take a stand
Never Judge A Book By Its Color
Open it and read it, my man.

THE BEGINNING

WWW.FACEBOOK.COM
COMMENTS

Levi Little January 10 at 9:35am

Unique, read thru your book. The one about mom got me - I'll say no more. Yourself titled open wall "Bloody Poetry" is one of my favs. No doubt you are a def poet. I like your "open wall" (open mic) theme for your page and I see your fan base growing. Not sure if you are, but if not, it may be time to get published. I use this service by Amazon for music, but they have a sweet deal for authors such as yourself who may want fans to grab their book off the shelf.

Much success to you in all that you do. Levi

Shawn Goddard January 12 at 6:39pm

i would be honored to share it, i really like the poems you wrote, let me know when the book comes out, keep me posted , use my wall to do what you need to do, its all about being a blessing , facebook has to have purpose , and my purpose is to encourage people , pray for them and just be a blessing, skies the limit to you Unique go to the next level

Deborah Upchurch January 10 at 2:19pm

Hi, we don't know each other, we have one mutual friend in common. I had to send you this message. Your "Book of Poetry" is absolutely amazing!!!! Keep them coming

Nefertiti Nef January 6 at 3:18pm

Unique, I only got to page 19 so far!! but this is deep, my favorite so far is Rest in Peace, it touched me and My heart in the palm of your hands deep cause I was just feelin that way a couple of months ago and I had to tell someone that!!! This ish is good, I would love to purchase a copy!! good stuff ;-) I also like how u put it 2gether, when u click on the pic & the poem find up. R u gonna get that in a book? I hope u do. I got one a couple of yrs ago, a book of poems. I hope u do. I will support ur work anytime!

Kathy Stokes January 5 at 10:19pm

Hey Unique, I started reading them when you first began to post them...i just read all of them from beginning to end and i think they are brilliant, It might sound weird but it seemed to be more than just words on a page, it was as if a scene was being acted out in my head as i read them...some of them hit home for me and kinda made me think about some things going on in my life so i appreciated that a lot! but like i said on your wall...keep writing, some people will like it some wont but everything ain't for everybody but just keep writing what's in your heart and mind and you WILL have a following!! I'll start the Unique Coles fan club..LOL!

Valerie Freeman January 6 at 5:57pm

Very impressive Unique. Who would have thought little Dondi bout to blow up. May God forever shine on you and through you, you have a gift that God blessed you with don't let anyone stop you from striving. I love you and I want the first copy. If there is anything I can do for you please do not hesitate to call me.

Peace and Love

Val

Pamela Brown YOU NEED TO PUT THIS IS WAX FOR THE WORLD TO ADHERE TOO...STOP CHEATING YOURSELF OF YOUR GIFT, THESE ARE WORDS OF ENCOURAGEMENT THAT OTHERS NEED TO HERE, YOUR WORK CAN DELIVER THAT LIFE CHANGING MESSAGE FOR SOME OF US THAT ARE GOING THROUGH TRIALS AND TRIBULATIONS AND NEED TO HEAR ENCOURAGING WORDS TO GIVE THEM THAT MOTIVATION TO MOVE ON......MAKE IT HAPPEN !

Jackie Burgess Salmond i truly believe the pain that we experience in the lost of a love one. will take time to heal, @ desarie yes they are our heavenly angels that why they were called home GOD needed them more than we did, Unique you have this talent for a reason GOD will have u to speak to people who's dealing with life's changes daily so keep it moving, much love

Dorcas Pitts WOW I am definitely impressed, Ur words have truly touched me deep within my soul, my Mom left me 21 yrs ago and my Dad 25 days, One thing I've learned from my Mom passing is it does get easier but u never lose the desire to have them in ur life. God bless and keep u, glad to see how well ur doing...1

Keisha Mckay **WOW this is wonderful this has touched my soul, it is so nice it brought tears to my eyes, god bless you and keep doing what you do, i am sure your mom is proud of you**

Camisa Oliver **Straight from your mouth to the ghettos ears, nice and real**

William Allen Hall **instant CLASSIC BOOOOIIIIIIIIII !!!**

Malinda Easton **God has given you a special talent!--I would def purchase--Keep us posted---Thxs for sharing!!**

The author touches on very serious subject matters that effects our everyday lives. If you can't relate to anything in this book, than you must not be of this world. There's something in this book that everybody can relate to. If you haven't gone through it yourself, you know someone else who did. These are more then just words on paper, it's literally "poetry in motion". The writer draws a very clear picture through out all of his poetry. So you're not only reading what the writer has written, you are also seeing what he's written. And no matter the age, sex, race or religion, after reading "Never Judge A Book By Its Color" you will never look at poetry the same. Unique Coles has just taken poetry to a whole 'nother level. This brilliant book of poetry is guaranteed to keep your attention from the beginning to the end. Whoever thought that poetry can be this entertaining?

Meet The Creative Team

Unique Coles
Author/Poet

Unique is an avid "B-Boy"; since the ripe age of 14. Born
and bred in Paterson, New Jersey's infamous "C.C.P."
projects. Unique has seen his share of drugs, money and
violence. Fed up with his battle with the legal system,
Unique decided to take his gift for writing, serious. Taking
his hometown by storm (winning talent shows, etc.) Unique
earned a reputation for being the "Lyrical Assassin"!
Influences like the Cold Crush Brothers, and KRS-1
motivated Unique to use his gift as a way out of his
environment. In 1995 he collaborated with a few local
rappers and hit the studio; after the company went
defunct, Unique was forced to retreat back to the streets,
only to end up yet again into the legal system.
Fast forward to the present, Unique is on a passionate
mission to use his gifts to bring his lyrical prowess to
the entertainment industry. Armed with a "Unique" style of
rhyming, and a bag full of "Unique" tricks up his
sleeves, you'll never know what's coming next. This

unpredictable, lyrical genius is guaranteed to take the industry by storm. Be on the look-out for future recordings, and literature from the "Unique" prowess of this gifted, all around writer!

Omar Wilkerson
Creative Consultant/Marketing
oglorious@hotmail.com

Omar Wilkerson was born in Cleveland Ohio. At the age of 5, his life has really taken a turning point after his mom passed. Having no father to step up to the plate; Omar lived in different states and relied on different family members to compliment his upbringing. At the age of 16 Omar discovered that he has a gift in poetry. After entering one of his poems into a poetry contest and receiving 1st place poet laureate reward; for his grade level; he felt a little bit more confident about his gift. As years progressed, Omar really discovered a deep love and appreciation for poetry after his aunt became a victim of violent crime. He wrote a poem called One More Chance. Currently, Omar performs for churches, spoken word venues and many other businesses who appreciate his material.

Unique and Omar has been the best of friends since 02. Omar is inspired by Unique for his creative ability to write. Unique is inspired by Omar for his "go get it" drive towards whatever it is he's pursuing. Together there are a great team. Omar is also in the process of putting together his own book of poetry. Be on the look out for that. They're also working on a couple of stage plays, "The Story of the People" from the essay in the book and also "Never Judge A Book By Its Color" stage play. This is just the beginning. There's so much more to come from these 2 God driven individuals. Stay tuned......

Elise Tiralli

diqitalxkarma@aol.com

**Graphic designer of,
"Bloody Poetry"**

Elise Tiralli (often called 'Lise' or 'E') was born November 14, 1992. She began practicing graphic design in early 2000, learning on her own and through website tutorials. Elise will graduate from Highland Regional Highland School in June 2011 and plans to attend college in September. She plans to pursue a career in Psychology with a double major in Italian Studies, but still intends to play around with graphic design in her spare time.

Marlon Majette
marlonmajette@rocketmail.com

**The artist of,
"Living in the drug world"**

I do not believe in overloaded an image, while conveying simplicity will bring out the true beauty of a picture. My art work makes a statement of "power" while being unique and sophisticated. When people look at my artwork, I want them to come away with a complete story that seeps out from the lines of the drawings. I hope you decide to add my work in your home, office and a place into your heart. I am committed to staying true to my art form and furthering my artistic vision. I believe that god has truly "blessed" me with undeniable talent and plan to use it to encourage and captivate people from many different walks of life.

Website: **http://marlonmajette.com**

Tony Lasala
Book/Sound Track Cover Designer
sobe2tone@yahoo.com

Tony Lasala is a Freelance Graphic Designer and Artist living in New Jersey. This project could not have been completed without his special touch.

You can see more of Tony's work at http://www.coroflot.com/multitone/Portfolio1/1.

Karen Foote
Booking Agent
exposed2fashion@yahoo.com

An accomplished Author, of The Guiding Light Daily Devotional Journal..A Woman of strong character, wisdom, faith and great compassion. Successful entrepreneur, a socially concerned educator. A leader who leads by example. Down to earth yet Kingdom minded, real talk, great sense of humor. Has a strong foundation based on the word of God. Daily pursuing the vision of God for her life.

http://www.exposed2fashion.com

The song "What If" will be
available on download as a gift.

"What If" produced by MD

Email me at
www.bloodypoetry4uni@yahoo.com

Also watch for the Play
**"Never Judge
A Book By Its Color"**

Follow Us:

www.bloodypoetry4uni.com
www.bloodypoetry4uni@yahoo.com
Facebook: http://www.facebook.com/justuniek
Twitter: @justuniek